SUPERC...

your Solar Sales

Get More Solar Leads

Using Free Internet Tools

by

EJ Thornton

Solar-Proud.com/books

ISBN: 9798519038577

Phone: (303) 794-8888

Books To Believe In

BooksToBelieveIn.com

solar-proud.com/books

Cover Art: ID 116464799 © Mulikov

Dedication

To everyone I've ever worked with in solar -

Past, present & future!

Your contribution to the planet

is appreciated!

Table of Contents

Introduction

Let your fingers do the walking...

There's an old slogan from the days of the old phone books to "Let Your Fingers Do the Walking". It just meant - that it was easier to call than it was to walk somewhere. It was more time-efficient as well.

The phone book is one thing - and the Internet is quite something else - with so much more power than an old paper copy of phone numbers.

One of the best ways to get solar leads is to knock doors... Why?

One reason is, it is easy to get to a whole bunch of potential leads in a short period of time. It just takes a minute or two to check a door - and only a couple of minutes more if someone answers and you can personalize the encounter using their own information. So in the span of an hour or so, you can reach a dozen or more households.

Solar - like most sales careers - is a numbers game, and once you realize that - you know you just have to put up the numbers to get the results.

So, what if I could show you a way - that you could talk to the same people whose doors you would have knocked - without ever leaving your home? I can teach you to create a set of leads that is geographically-centered, with which you already have a connection, so they'll open up that proverbial door to you and to solar.

That is what this book is about - teaching you to get your numbers up using free Internet tools with a set of leads that is statistically known to close at a higher percentage than door-knocked or canvassed leads.

Using these free Internet tools in a strategic combination allows you to just let your fingers do the walking through a neighborhood - quickly and efficiently.

Sound good?

Who is this book for?

This is written for solar sales consultants.

If you sell residential solar and are responsible in any way, shape or form for your own leads, this book is for you!

This information will expand your reach as far as you want to reach. It will turn one lead into 6 if you follow the 6-pack method. It will jump start your referrals and make great ambassadors out of your customers.

If you give someone a fish -

you feed them for a day -

if you teach them how to fish,

you feed them for a lifetime.

I hope - in my way - this is teaching you how to fish in an amazingly large ocean that has plenty of fish to choose from and we all make great livings while we help more people "Go Green" by installing solar.

What this book is not

This book assumes you have a basic knowledge of solar sales and basic computer talent.

I'm not setting out here to teach you how to do solar sales, instead I'm hoping that getting you more qualified referral leads, you'll be able to increase your solar sales success rate. So basic solar sales knowledge is assumed.

Technically, I expect that you know how to type in a URL to go to a website, and to know how to use your cell phone for texting and phone calls.

If we're good on those skills - then you're ready!

If you're not good on those, contact the author for solar sales basic training via her company's mentor program and then we can take next steps.

URL: https://solar-proud.com/ej   **(select "JOIN")**

About EJ Thornton

I've been in the solar business for decades - literally - my father was a solar engineer. He designed massive solar power plants back in the 1970s and 1980s.

I'm 2nd generation solar!

**My dad (far right) in 1984
my husband - 2nd from the left
working with his amazing crew!**

I've been solar-aware for decades and I've seen the industry blossom from just 'the true believers' to what it is today, a huge industry poised to make a real environmental difference.

I've also had residential solar on my home since 2016.

Being the daughter of the afore-mentioned engineer, a mathematician myself and married to a computer programmer, I can assure you that I've graphed and logged my experience with my own solar system every which way I possibly could.

My house - "Solar Proud" since 6/1/2016

I decided to take a job in residential solar sales in March of 2017. Using my mathematics background, I systemized the solar sales process - very quickly becoming the best sales person the company had produced. In 2018, I sold over $2.1 million dollars in residential solar - reaching the threshold to make "President's Club" at my solar company. I outpaced every one of my fellow solar sales co-workers there by over 30%.

What made me different - not better - just different, is that I looked at the solar sales process from a system's perspective and was able to capitalize on it.

I quit that company in 2019, and struck out on my own. I now work for a large very progressive solar company, where I am a solar sales independent contractor and mentor.

I've built tools - above and beyond what was provided to me by any company. Those tools helped me sell more solar and gain referral business. I still use and teach them in my solar sales business today.

Solar, as an industry is on the precipice of amazing growth. I want to see ethical and talented people get ahead in it. So, I teach my insights to others with the hope that I can help them excel in their careers.

Best to you all!

Let the sun shine in!!!

Warning
The dangers of using "free" Internet tools

Not everything is really free...
When you use free Internet tools.
There is always a catch.

Maybe the catch is to show you how good their data is, just to create a demand for what the site has, and then upsell you to a paid membership or a paid service.

Maybe the site puts a cookie on your machine so that they can track your interests and then you'll see ads for this service and others like it on Social Media. You can almost count on this to happen.

In some cases, where personal data is on a free site on the Internet, the catch is the only way to remove your data off of it costs money. That might be the whole reason the site exists in the first place.

This free data comes from online public sources that these free sites scrape. All the data is out on the Internet - and you could get it yourself without using this site - if you just knew where to look. But these sites assemble this information for you in a convenient easy-to-use format.

That much data freely accessible online is somewhat chilling. What you can find out about someone is downright scary. But the information that a solar sales rep needs to find out to create a lead is very surface level - and available on these free sites.

You don't have to dig into other public records to find out things about your prospects.

The other catch is accuracy, or up-to-date information. These public data sites exist for their own purposes - *not your benefit.* So there are no guarantees that this information is accurate or even relevant today. Verifying the data you find on these sites is necessary.

Approach cautiously!

Beware clicking around on too many other buttons. There could be fees involved. The following lessons are all about how to use the **free tools** available online to generate sales leads - nothing more.

Chapter 1

Don't Buy Leads

When you can get them yourself...

**It's easy -
and the information is free
and right in front of you.**

As soon as you let people know you're in residential solar sales hoping to get leads, the first thing you find out is there are a ton of people out there willing to sell you thousands upon thousands of leads - or create a lead magnet for you for just a few thousand dollars a month to maintain.

Just go put the word **solar** on your profile at LinkedIn or on Facebook and watch how quickly ads start popping up from solar lead companies or how quickly your LinkedIn messenger blows up with personal messages with people hoping to connect with you to make you more successful... for a price!

The beauty of the solar industry is that it is really lucrative <u>but everyone else knows it too</u>, so they just assume you're willing to pay... Because they make it sound so easy!

The hardest part about the solar industry is the lead flow.

When companies start adding up the costs of a canvassing team, a phone team or a trade show team, you can see why the value of a vetted solar lead out there has a hefty price tag.

As an independent solar sales rep, you can't compete with that - nor should you try. Whether you work for a company or are a 1099ed sales rep for a mega-solar company, you probably don't have the resources to develop a team for lead generation - not at first anyway.

So these lead-generation companies approach you - and they sound kinda good. With as lucrative as solar can be, just one good sale can make up for all these up-front investments - even month after month after month…

**But why spend that good money,
when you can create your own leads
using free and easy Internet tools?**

If you just knew where to go…

But that is what I'm here to teach you!

Solar is a numbers game, and unlike other trades that are sold to homeowners, you can instantly tell if a house is good for solar. So you can literally do all the canvassing you need to do from right in front of your computer screen.

Remember, you only need a few sales a month to make your life really sweet.

This is really powerful information. Like one of my mentors in digital marketing always asks his readers - make me a promise - right now - that you'll only use this for good.

If you can't make me that promise, return this for a full refund!

Cool - you're still with me!

Let's get started...

Chapter 2

Referrals are the best

Or are they?

Everyone who has ever been in sales has raved about how "customer referral" business is great.

The fact that "Customer-referred deals close at a much higher rate than non-referred leads" is often cited as the main reason why everyone wants to pursue customer-referrals.

Often - solar companies reward sales reps with a higher commission if they bring in their own referral business.

So they train you...

They train you in strong-arm techniques to get your customers to give you names and numbers.

One popular one is to just sit in silence after you put an empty form in front of the customer you just pitched. You ask your customer to take out their cell phone and just 'scroll' through it right then and fill it out. Then you just sit there and wait - and don't say anything until he/she complies with you - or throws you out.

These techniques can turn allies into enemies -

I've been able to get referrals like this - but more times than not, I've been conned by my customer because they gave me fake names and numbers. Or they gave me names of people they don't really know.

No one likes to be strong-armed. You've probably just turned them into someone who would never refer someone to you because they don't want their friends to be strong-armed either.

**Most people want to vette the lead first,
then release the name to the sales person.**

If I ditch the strong-arm techniques, and I just simply ask for what I want, - a referral - I get many people telling me that they're willing to refer people to me. **BUT...** they're hesitant to give their contact information out. They want to ask the other person's permission before they feel comfortable giving their name out. I get that - it's considerate. I'd do the same.

Have you ever had someone say, "I bet Joe would love this - but let me call him first to make sure it's okay for you to call." They never call Joe - and you never get the referral. Worse yet - your customer never gets that valuable referral bonus.

Or the best excuse in solar, since it is a several week process to go from sale to install - the customer says, "I'll give you names once I know if I like the process or not." That's reasonably logical - and hard to overcome, but again, it is just an excuse to get rid of you.

But worst of all - what if they don't actually know the contact info... How do you overcome that? Plain and simply - you don't!

* * *

What if, instead, you could sit down in front of someone you just pitched - explain the referral bonus opportunity with them, then produce a piece of paper with several names of people they should know, with the contact information already obtained. Then you could just ask your customer about these people without having your customer having to produce any information.

Imagine asking instead, "Joe here is your next door neighbor. His house is prime for solar too. When I call him, is it okay to tell him we talked first?"

So now, they know you already have the contact information.

They didn't give the information out, so they don't have to worry about getting an irate call from Joe about compromising his phone number. They also already know you're going to call Joe - with or without their permission. What they'll quickly come to realize is that if they say not to use their name, they'll not be entitled to the referral bonus you've just made them excited about.

What do you think they'll say? You know what? It doesn't really matter - you're still going to call Joe!

Think about it... Unlike common strong-arm tactics, this technique provides a win/win/win for you - your customer and for the referral.

Using the tools I'm about to teach you,
you'll be able to create that exact
win/win/win scenario.

You'll have access to the names and numbers of tons of people, so your referral partner won't have to give them to you. You'll simply go down a list - and ask about the people, and get some good insight as to how to sell them. You'll already know who they are.

Helping your customer to provide you their first few referrals does many things for you:

1. It shows them that you're serious about solar , so it builds your credibility

2. You're helping them, it shows you're generous and caring

3. It teaches them how to use your referral process, so when they independently think of someone to refer to you, they already know the process.

It's basic physics...

An object in motion - tends to stay in motion, and an object at rest tends to stay at rest. If you can get them moving, they'll tend to stay that way.

Once the customer gets a referral bonus or two - it's a safe bet, more and more of their contact list will suddenly be available to you.

Chapter 3

Start with an anchor address

Geographically grouping your leads comes with many benefits.

The first thing you need is an address. The easiest one to choose is one of your customers or referral partners - maybe someone you sold already or maybe the guy you're just about to go pitch.

But what if you're new to solar and don't have any prospects yet?

Use your own home.

Use a family member's home

Choose a hot neighborhood.

What makes a hot neighborhood? You decide

* Lots of solar already - so those neighbors see solar all the time - "Solar social proof" has already been accomplished

* Gated neighborhood - one that no one can canvass in person - prime territory

* Houses on big lots that no one would canvass because the houses are so far apart

* A densely packed neighborhood with lots of single family homes

Who knows - you choose what you choose for the reasons that make the most sense to you.

Once you have your anchor address: enter it into google maps.

Go to **maps.Google.com** - and look around the neighborhood.

If you don't know the exact address - then start with the cross streets and work your way to your optimum house.

Enter the anchor address - or find the house on the map to get the anchor address.

Look at all the information this single image is giving you right now!

The street is labelled, the house number is clearly visible. The neighbor's house numbers are also visible. (If you don't see a house number in Google Maps, click on the house, and it will appear).

These house numbers are the clue to the next level of information you can access!

Chapter 4

Get the 6-pack

Curious neighbors are a gold mine!

Many solar companies teach their sales rep to go out to the home of the customer on the day of the solar install - and visit each neighbor saying something like, "We're doing an install over here on Bill's house today. If you need anything or have any questions, call me - here's my card." The hope is that the customer will be curious enough about the install to make a phone call to you. This has a small amount of success - but why wait until the day of install to introduce yourself to these people?

The neighbors on each side of the anchor address and the 3 across the street create "the 6-pack."

Instead of waiting until Bill's install is underway, you can introduce yourself to these people right away. Find out who they are - before you go and pitch Bill.

You've got their addresses - that was the easy part.

Now what?

We'll say that Bill lives at 16332 Goldenrod Pl., Louisville KY. You can see his two next-door neighbors live at 16316 Goldenrod Pl, Louisville KY, and 16348 Goldenrod Pl, Louisville KY. And his 3 neighbors across the street have house numbers of 16315, 16331, and 16347.

Below is a worksheet that you can use to track this. To request a PDF copy of the worksheet that you can print yourself, visit **solar-proud.com/tools** - and we'll email one to you.

Referral Worksheet For: _

Personalized Link:_____

Address:

Phone(s):

Address: _____

Name(s): _____

Phone(s): _____

Notes: _____

Notes:

Address: _____

Name(s): _____

Phone(s): _____

Notes: _____

Address:

Name(s):

Phone(s):

Notes:

Get your downloadable file at:
Solar-Proud.com/tools

Address: _____

Name(s): _____

Phone(s): _____

Notes: _____

_____

_____

_____

Address: _____

Name(s): _____

Phone(s): _____

Notes: _____

_____

_____

_____

Disclaimer:

This is some powerful information we are about to share - and if you think of its ramifications - it can be some scary stuff - so remember the promise you made to only use this for good? I'm going to hold you to it!

I did not create these free websites - I have no stake in these websites - and there are many more of these than what will be discussed here. So, if suddenly, one of these websites quit working, there will be others that do.

Chapter 5

Is it a good house for solar?

**Unlike lead gen for other trades,
it is easy to tell from a satellite map
if a house is good for solar - or not.**

All you have to do to get the full address of each of those houses is to click on the house itself - and the address will appear in the search bar of google.

Verify that solar will work on the house!

Before you bother to put a house on your list, check the house first for good roof slopes for solar - check the shading of the area, etc.

Google Maps is a good place to start, but you can also use Google's Solar Lead Gen site, "Project Sunroof" to see if it is a good house for solar.

https://maps.google.com

This house is a great candidate for solar!

http://google.com/sunroof

The brighter the yellow on the roof, the more sun it gets!

You can see how shading affects the colors using this tool. Even though the house in the middle is next door to a couple of great solar houses, it is not a great solar house - unless they cut some trees down. Again, something to talk about with your prospect. Don't assume this tool has the latest pictures on it. It is pretty reliable, but not necessarily up-to-date.

Be aware, this isn't just an information tool for google - it is a lead generation site for them, so use it carefully - but don't generally let your customers loose on it. If they scroll to the bottom of the page, they just might become someone else's customer.

Once you become a seasoned solar pro - you'll be able to tell just by looking at the roofline if it is a good home for solar or not - with or without the Project Sunroof.

Chapter 6

How long have these neighbors lived in that house?

Real Estate sites tell you what you need to know.

Now that you have the addresses in hand, find out what you can. You'll be amazed at how much information is out on the Internet when you have someone's address.

Your next step: **the real estate websites:** Check Zillow or RedFin to find out how long these neighbors have lived in those houses - or if those houses are up for sale. These little tidbits will be great conversations starters when you actually reach out to these people.

Enter the address on these sites and watch the houses come up.

For example, based on the clearly visible phrase "Off market", you can see this house isn't up for sale at the moment. If a house is listed for sale, scratch it off the list or put it on a call back list for 6 months from now.

⌂ Zillow

✎ Edit   ♡ Save

3 bd | 3 ba | 1,599 sqft

● Off market | Zestimate®: **$449,229** | Rent Zestin

Est. refi payment: $1,948/mo Ⓢ **Refinance your loan**

Home value   Owner tools   Home details   Neighbo

Similar homes nearby
Avg. sold price: $414,650 | **Avg. $/Square Feet:** $213

The 1599 sqft tidbit is the most valuable piece of information on this screen especially if you established that someone had just moved into the house! We'll get to the reason why a little later.

Now scroll down a bit to get to the Pricing & Tax History.

Price and tax history

Price history

Date	Event	Price	
3/3/1998	Sold	$149,800 (+12.6%)	$94/sqft
Source: Public Record Report			
4/30/1996	Sold	$133,000	$83/sqft
Source: Public Record Report			

You can see someone has owned this house since 1998.

We don't know yet if this is a good property for solar. For instance, this might be an investment property with renters inside. But if we can establish that this is owner-occupied, again, the fact that they've been there since 1998 is some interesting information that you can use to help the owners understand the value of solar.

How much have they already sent to the utility?

If you can establish when they moved in, you can calculate by reverse engineering their usage - approximately how much money they've already wasted by sending it to the utility… *(See "calculator" chapter).*

Is the house old enough to have outdated electric panel issues?

Pay attention to the year the home was built, especially if you are working in a place where they used electrical boxes that now force a main panel upgrade. The more prepared you are for questions like that on the initial call, the more impressed these prospects are going to be with your knowledge of solar.

If there was a new sale listed (less than 3 months), then you can use the square foot information to base your proposal… *(See "calculator" chapter).*

Knowledge is power!

Chapter 7

Who lives there now?

Public data sites are the new "phone book."

You can see from Zillow that someone has owned this house since 1998.

But what if we could get the names, ages and phone numbers of the people who live there now? If we could get that information ourselves, our customer wouldn't have to give it to us. That major objection of getting the other people's permission has been cleared!

This is the beauty of these websites, we can do just a little investigating and come up with some amazing information.

Public Records Encyclopedia

Learn all about any address, person or company in the US without leaving your couch. ClustrMaps.com makes finding information in the United States easier than ever.

Address   People   Company

Address   **Find**

Widgets served since 2005   12,511,771,496

https://clustrmaps.com

Right now my favorite for this is <u>clustrmaps.com</u>. But don't get too attached to it, it might be gone tomorrow. I've used several of these types of sites over the years to do this kind of work, and they come and they go.

On clustrmaps, you can enter an address - and press "Find" - and then you get a list of the people who lived at that address.

These sites scour and scrape information from many public data sources such as state and county records. Then they assemble all the different pieces and display it together. Most of the time, it's correct - but sometimes it's not.

My personal information actually went back to addresses that I had back to my college days in 1984. So, it is a wealth of information.

However, sometimes these sites have the wrong information. One of the addresses listed for my brother was clearly mistaken - in the wrong state, married to another woman… Maybe he's leading a double life, but more likely, the site just matched up data incorrectly..

**So, understand - this is free data,
assembled from public sources.**

It could also be out of date...

It may or may not be accurate. I've found this to be accurate enough when paired with google and Zillow that I've been able to use it to do what I'm teaching you. I'm just cautioning you - to do your own due diligence.

Enter a house address in the search bar - and prepare to be amazed!

Here's an example...

100 W Wesley

wood

Known Residents

Aimee Kim

Details

Age 48
(   ) 736-2605

David S

Details

Age 49
(   ) 916-9404

The property owner's name is   David S. Ownership information for the parcel
302079272(links this address to   David S. The building was erected in 2005. The property is sixteen years old, which is 33 years younger than the average age of a building in Lakewoo of 49 years. The size of the land lot is 21,462 sqft. The building is one story high. The house is zoned a: a single family residence. The property was valued at $633,493 on Nov 12, 2004. The house is located on the parcel #492840   . It has three bedrooms. According to the plan, there are three full baths. The price per sqft for this home is $222.7. This is a single floor house. The house's living area is 2,845 sqft. The structure type can be characterized as Ranch. The heating type was specified as forced air. As for parking options, they are as follows: attached garage, 3 spaces, 844 sqft garage. The ZIP code for this address is 8022   and the postal code suffix is 3070. The   neighborhood contains this property. 39.6   ,-105.1   are the coordinates for the property. Residents of 80227 pay approximately $1,570 a month for a 2-bedroom unit. HUD says fair market rent for a 2-bedroom apartment in .   County is $1,605

What can we glean from this information that's pertinent to solar?

We can see that there are two residents - David and Aimee - and that David owns the house. The house was built in 2005 - which is likely also found on the real estate websites. You can verify the square footage of the house here too.

But the best thing you can see is that there are phone numbers for both David and Aimee - and ages listed. You can tell quickly that these guys are in a very viable age group for buying solar and that this house is owner-occupied.

That's all we need to know for this exercise.

Collect David and Aimee's phone numbers and put them on the list of possibles to have your customer confirm that he'd be okay if you called.

It's that simple.

You can get the neighbor's contact information without our customer having to look it up.

So, when you are going to approach a new client, and you want to turn them into a referral partner - do a little homework first.

Go to google with their address as the anchor address

* Verify their home

* Get the six pack

* Verify the houses are good for solar

* Verify the houses are owner-occupied

* Get the names and phones from clustrmaps.com

* Present a fully filled out list of neighbors for your client.

Ask your client how well they know the neighbors and if he/she is okay using their name to begin the conversation.

Record that information - especially if your customer tells you something pertinent about that neighbor.

Contact the neighbors, sell them solar too and send your client referral bonus checks -

Check back in on your happy client - and see who else he knows.

The point here is to help our referral partners along - get them past the stumbling block of having to surrender their friends list to a sales person. But even more important, if we do our job properly, not only are we creating more sales and commission for ourselves, we're helping our customers by getting them more referral bonuses.

If we can jumpstart our referrers into success, the list of referrals will be unlimited and bountiful.

I wish you the best of luck - and please, use this information responsibly. Use it to forward the cause of solar and make our planet greener for all of us.

Chapter 8

How do you find the decision makers?

Logical guidelines *generally* get you to the right people.

To sell solar, you need to talk to the decision makers of the household. In the above example, where there were only two people listed, they were approximately the same age. You can deduce that this is a couple and that they are the decision makers of the household. But it isn't always that easy.

Consider the following household...

This is a house that has 9 people listed. Clearly one is a duplicate (again free data - is free).

Known Residents

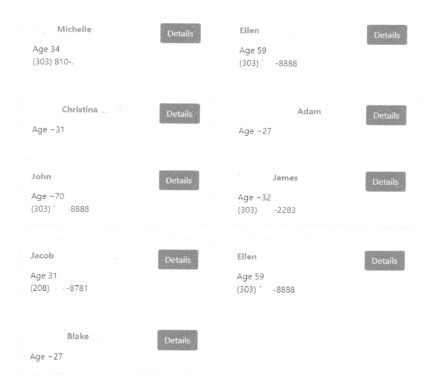

Michelle
Age 34
(303) 810-.
[Details]

Ellen
Age 59
(303) ˙ -8888
[Details]

Christina _ :
Age ~31
[Details]

Adam
Age ~27
[Details]

John
Age ~70
(303) ˙ -8888
[Details]

James
Age ~32
(303) -2283
[Details]

Jacob
Age 31
(208) ·-8781
[Details]

Ellen
Age 59
(303) ˙ -8888
[Details]

Blake
Age ~27
[Details]

But here, you can tell that there are two people in the house that are roughly 20-30 years older than the rest. You can guess that John and Ellen are probably the decision makers. It isn't always the oldest people in the house though, so use logic and discernment when trying to deduce this.

A little further down, you see this:

John   owns this real estate property. The size of
property was $251,000. This is a single family residence
house on Nov 2, 2006 was at $251,000. #20733240211
there are four bedrooms. This home features three full
There are two levels. The house's living area is 1,846 sc
approximate length of the perimeter is 322 ft. The list
building includes wood. It has a composition roof. The
parking options, they are as follows: attached garage,

John ..... owns this real estate property.

Owner-occupied - _check_!

So you have just verified that John is the decision maker. It looks like he might be the only one on title - so by most standards, we can consider him the decision maker.

Find out if there is another decision maker in the home. Scan the list by age. There is someone else approximately John's age - likely his wife. Assume two decision makers in this house. If there is a different phone number for this second decision maker, then you have another potential phone number for this address.

Chapter 9

How do you handle a rental property?

Check the names against the ownership

What if - when you read a little further down, you see this:

XYZ Trust ..... owns this real estate property.

A company owns the property - not an individual. Is it a rental? You don't know just from that bit of information. It could also be a "trust" - and the house is still technically owner-occupied.

It is very likely a rental if it is owned by someone who is not ever listed as a resident.

Who is the decision maker then? It will always be whoever owns the house.

Rentals have some advantages
if you can find the owner

There are more tax deductions available to someone who puts solar on a rental property - but this book is not the place to teach you those. If you choose to go after landlords as prospects, learn the tax implications of investment properties before you pitch.

Chapter 10

Do Not Call List

You're still bound by this!!!

I know the savvy sales rep is going to see far more potential in these tools than just increasing referral success.

I've used this technique to 'phone canvass' neighborhoods where I didn't have an introduction from a neighbor.

This has one more layer of due diligence. Because you're calling strangers - you have to abide by the "Do not call" list.

The "Do not call" list rule does not apply to referrals, because you have someone who in effect has made the introduction, but it does apply if you're just going to use a random house as your anchor address to call or create a list.

The phone numbers can be verified against the Do not call registry using the website:

https://www.donotcall.gov/verify.html

There are other verification websites for the Do Not Call lists - just do a search - and vette them before you use them.

Learn the restrictions of the TCPA: Telephone Consumer Protection Act - and the GDPR: General Data Protection Regulation.

Chapter 11

What else can you tell?

Again - knowledge is power.

However, trivia is trivia - learn to tell the difference!

If you're going to dig deep in a neighborhood, you might want to know the age demographic of it as well. The following is a graph, from clustrmaps of my neighborhood and its age distribution.

This kind of information might help you prepare your pitch better.

Neighbors' Age Distribution

The graph shows the distribution of age groups in the neighborhood based on data for the 500 households located nearby

18-25 years	3.3%
25-35 years	17.4%
35-45 years	32%
45-65 years	38.7%
65-90 years	8.4%

Chapter 12

Leave your anchor-address' customer with a link they can post on social media

If you're going to post on social media, you've got to have a personal link where the leads that come in from it land in your back office, *not just the general company lead site.*

My first solar company did not understand this - and kept asking us to post the company's website on our personal social media, but with no accountability that the leads we generated would be assigned to us. It was a crazy thing to ask employees to do - and basically no one did it, because it wasn't worth anything to us.

So, I created my own system for collecting referrals - and not just for me, but I created this for each one of my referral partners. Everyone who posts for me in social media is credited with the lead that comes in from it. A personalized trackable link is critical in this day and age to create more referrals.

If you create a social media post, and you can tag the customer in it so it appears in their newsfeed on social media, and it comes with a personalized link, you better believe the savvy customer will share that post, and tag their friends. You've just expanded your reach to all of their social media network.

Luckily, my new company understands this and has a robust 'ambassador' program for this very thing. So for that I'm grateful. I do still have my personal system that creates links for solar sales reps and their referral partners for those many, many of us out there that need it.

If you want to create more referrals, make it easy for your partners to refer to you. Social media is one amazing pathway to more business.

Chapter 13

Keep in touch with milestone metrics

One very easy way to get more referrals is to reach back across your sold projects and re-connect with them. And then once you've reconnected, use the 6-pack method to start them referring their friends to you.

I use SendOutCards.com application, but you can use anything as long as it creates snail mail that they can post on their refrigerator. I create custom greeting cards to send to my customers for many reasons. I send "Thank You" notes after a sale. I send a "Congrats, You're Solar Powered" card after PTO (Permission to Operate). I send them 'Solar Birthday" cards once a year with their milestone statistics on it.

Solar Milestones:

This send-out application calculator is for "sold" customers with kWhs already produced. Based on the install date, size of the system and current cost of power, an attractive image is created explaining the energy savings, cost savings, pollution savings and equivalent tree metric. These images are suitable for customer correspondence or social media posts.

Each of my physical greeting cards has contact information on the back that keeps my name and number close at hand for my customers.

After I send the card, I call a couple of weeks later to see if they got it - and then we catch up. It is then I ask how they're doing. If it is good, then I ask them for referrals. If they're not doing good, I don't.

If their solar system has trouble, we'll fix that first. If they're not doing well for other reasons, I'm respectful of them as people and not ask them for anything at that point.

But I will put them on my calendar to call back at hopefully a better time when I can ask.

As far as images go, I also post them on Facebook and tag my customer in them. What that does is the image appears in their feed, and their friends see an attractive picture with a personalized solar message on it. I put the customer's personal link on the post as well, such that if anyone clicks on it, the customer gets credit for the referral.

My husband is an FAA licensed drone pilot, so we often provide nice aerial photos of our customer's solar roofs. Occasionally, for a small fee, we "drone" roofs for others too. These photos are awesome for social media purposes too. You might know a local person who can provide this service for you.

Learn to think "Outside the box" for other ideas.

If you take the time to get each customer's personal referral engine started, it will pay off major dividends in the long run.

Chapter 14

Other ideas to help you find 'hot' anchor addresses

County databases for recent home improvement permits.

It's okay if you don't have the homeowner's name - you have their address on the permit - and you have the name of the contractor. That provides us even more potential...

New Roofs - did a hail storm just go through your area?

If so, there are going to be a slew of 're-roof' permits going through your county permit site, which is also online. You can get a list of them, and that can be your intro to finding an anchor address in a neighborhood.

Finished basements/construction additions - when homeowners do home renovations, usually they add electricity demands to the house. It's a good time to reach out to them about their bill.

There are many other trades that need permits to do work with homeowners. The thing about permits is that the contractor will likely be the one who applies for the permit. Keep in mind, that you and the contractor share a mutual client type. Now, instead of these one-offs that you find in the permit database, you can approach the contractor directly to find a way to enlist them as your ambassador or to create another type of win/win opportunity for leads.

Warning:

Do not scour the permit databases for other solar permits and then go try to get that homeowner to cancel the job with the other company to go with you. That practice gives the whole solar industry a bad name, and makes you just as vulnerable for the next guy to steal your deal. Don't be that person!

Chapter 15

Equations and Calculators

solar-proud.com/calculators

In the solar industry, there are several opportunities to crunch numbers. You can look at solar deals from many angles and each utility's different rate structure forces the need for spreadsheets and calculators.

We have expertise in this field going back to the 70s - We have done efficiency calculations and cost-benefit analyses for massive solar fields that were the ancestors of what we have today. So we have decades of experience in this field. We have adapted many of those calculations to the residential solar model.

Try out the free Solar Milestone calculator.

See chapter 13

Solar Milestones:

This calculator is for existing solar customers with kWhs already produced.

Based on the install date, size of the system and current cost of power, an attractive image is created explaining the energy savings, cost savings, pollution savings and equivalent tree metric. These images are suitable for customer correspondence or social media posts.

If you like that...

We have created a membership site for access to many specialized solar calculators and training on how to use them. If you're interested in these calculators, visit solar-proud.com/tools and sign up for monthly membership.

List of calculators:

How much money have they already wasted?

If you can establish when they moved in, you can calculate by reverse engineering the average bill or the homeowner's usage - approximately how much money he's already wasted by sending it to the utility.

Square foot usage estimator:

If the homeowner is new to the residence (less than 3 months), then using the square footage to estimate usage is the best way to size a system. The calculations are based on the following article.

https://homeprofessionals.org/solar/average-kwh-usage-for-a-2000-sq-ft-home/ - article explaining how to calculate usage if only given square footage of a residence.

Estimating solar savings based on an average electric payment:

If you can't get an electric bill, but you can get an average monthly payment estimate from someone, then dazzle them with an approximate estimate of how much solar will save them over the next 25 years.

Estimate usage based on an average electric payment:

Based on the amount paid, and a known cost/kWh, you can estimate annual usage well enough to create a base proposal.

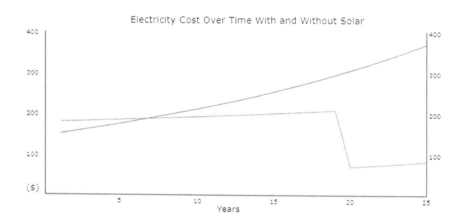

Electricity Cost Over Time With and Without Solar

Inflation comparison graph:

Based on current electric bill, predicted inflation, solar payment and offset, this quick graph shows how long until the total new solar payment is less than the electric payment - and how those payments compare over 25 or 30 years - with annual totals.

Remaining warrantied life of the panels:

Using the same parameters as the PVValue report, this calculator quickly generates an estimate of how much money your solar system will still offset future electricity bills. Where only official sites can claim an equity stake, this calculator will prove the solar system will save money on the electric bill - warrantied by the manufacturer.

How many more solar panels will you need if you buy an electric car?

With a few easy-to-find variables from your customer (how many miles they drive/year) - your proposal (how much production each solar panel adds) and the car manufacturer's information (how many kWh / 100 miles), you can easily calculate how much more solar production you'll need to add to cover adding an electric car to the current design.

And new tools and calculators are being created all the time.

Chapter 16

Other services

Automated lists of neighborhoods - up to 100 house addresses:

If you want an automated list of the houses near an anchor address, you can request that at the tools page.

$10 for 100.

Solar sales Speaking Engagements:

If you want me to teach your crew about how to use these Internet tools, any of the calculators we offer or some of our proprietory strategies, contact EJ at **ej@solar-proud.com** for more details.

Unique links for your referrers:

If your company doesn't offer a direct Internet link for you or your referrals to use in social media and emails that land those leads directly in your inbox, we will create a unique link for as many referrals as you would like for $10/link.

You and the referrer will get an email if anyone enters a lead after clicking on that link.

Geographically organized email addresses:

When you are a solar expert, focusing on specific geographical areas, gives you great advantages. You probably only have to know the particulars of one utility at a time. Here - geographically focused email campaigns can be extremely useful. Another idea on how to use a geographically-centered email list, is that Facebook can use the list to create a 'look-alike' list - and if the main thing the emails have in common, is a geographic area, you'll have a wider local reach!

If you want to buy geographically organized email lists by city and state, they're available here. This will allow you an unprecedented reach into a neighborhood, town or city.

Go to solar-proud.com/calculators to initiate requests for these services as well.

Chapter 17

Resources

Author's Solar Websites:

https://solar-proud.com/tools - sign up for access to the Solar Proud suite of tools.

https://solar-proud.com/calculators - varied and useful calculators for solar professionals.

https://www.facebook.com/solarproud - Solar Proud's facebook business page.

https://solar-proud.com/milestones/ - calculator to find savings to date on installed solar systems.

https://www.SendOutCards.com/u/ejthornton - Greeting card website. $97/month for unlimited UNIQUE greeting cards.

https://ejthornton.com/promos - Affordable advertising products to make for customers and prospects.

https://medium.com/solar-chronicles - Solar Chronicles - EJ Thornton's publication on Medium.com

Real Estate Websites to find out when the house was sold last:

Zillow.com

Redfin.com

Google Tools:

https://www.google.com/get/sunroof - Project Sunroof - analyses houses for solar efficiency - lead gen for google.

https://Maps.google.com - google maps tool

Recommended Websites:

https://Clustrmaps.com - getting the names, homeowners' and decision makers for an address

https://www.donotcall.gov/verify.html - verify if a phone number is on the Do Not Call List.

Summary

I've provided you with many tools, techniques and strategies to help you kick start your referral business. By doing a little research before your appointment, or before any new contact with a potential referral partner, you open the door for them by helping them - and helping them help you.

Using the free Internet tools, you can open up a neighborhood and create an advocate for a whole neighborhood. Showing them how easy it is to refer people and that there is nothing to fear or dread about it will remove any block in their way.

Strong-arm techniques get you names, but not advocates. Kickstarting your referral partner's success gets you referrals now - and for years to come.

Keeping in touch with your customers and creating customized links opens up all your referral partner's social media potential into your business.

Make them look good - and tag them, and they'll share and you'll get noticed. Let them know a little work (sharing) has a great reward, and you'll get people shouting your name from the mountaintop - figuratively.

Referrals are easy to get - and easy to keep flowing, but when you prime the pump in these positive ways, you'll see amazing success.

Good luck

& keep selling the sunshine!

Lightning Source UK Ltd.
Milton Keynes UK
UKHW021602101022
410237UK00013B/2280